Why Mommy is a Democrat

by
Jeremy Zilber

illustrated by
Yuliya Firsova

The author thanks Julia and Isabella Greenleaf for their encouragement and numerous contributions, Bill Hixon for his nonpartisan advice, and Joe and Judy Zilber for instilling strong Democratic principles at an early age.

This book is dedicated to the next generation of Democrats.

Copies of this book can be purchased at **www.littledemocrats.net**

At least 5% of the profits from the sale of this book will be donated to Democratic candidates and Democratic party organizations.

Printed in the United States of America.
Second Printing.
ISBN: 0-9786688-0-4

Some Mommies are called Democrats.

Your Mommy is a Democrat because…

Democrats make sure everyone always has enough to eat, just like Mommy does.

Democrats make sure everyone is treated fairly, just like Mommy does.

Democrats make sure everyone plays by the rules, just like Mommy does.

Democrats make sure no one just like Mommy does.

fights,

Democrats make sure we all share our toys, just like Mommy does.

Democrats
people
just like

make sure we are nice to
who are different,
Mommy does.

Democrats make sure sick
just like Mommy

people are able to see a doctor, does.

Democrats make sure we are always safe, just like Mommy does.

Democrats make sure
just like

we clean up our messes,
Mommy does.

Democrats make sure children can go to school, just like Mommy does.

Democrats make sure everyone has a warm bed to sleep in, just like Mommy does.

And that is why

Mommy is a Democrat!